JESUS>RELIGION

THE BIBLE STUDY

JEFFERSON BETHKE

D1303162

LifeWay Press®
Nashville, Tennessee

Published by LifeWay Press® • © 2014 Jefferson Bethke

No part of this book may be reproduced or transmitted in any form or by any means, electronic or mechanical, including photocopying and recording, or by any information storage or retrieval system, except as may be expressly permitted in writing by the publisher. Requests for permission should be addressed in writing to LifeWay Press®; One LifeWay Plaza; Nashville, TN 37234-0152.

ISBN 978-1-4300-2979-3 • Item 005615714

Dewey decimal classification: 248.84
Subject heading: CHRISTIAN LIFE \ FORGIVENESS \ GRACE (THEOLOGY)

To order additional copies of this resource, write to LifeWay Church Resources Customer Service; One LifeWay Plaza; Nashville, TN 37234-0113; fax 615.251.5933; phone toll free 800.458.2772; email *orderentry@lifeway.com;* order online at *www.lifeway.com;* or visit the LifeWay Christian Store serving you.

Printed in the United States of America

Adult Ministry Publishing • LifeWay Church Resources
One LifeWay Plaza • Nashville, TN 37234-0152

CONTENTS

ABOUT JEFFERSON

Hey, guys! The first time meeting someone is always awkward, so I thought I'd start by sharing a little bit about myself.

I was born in Tacoma, Washington.
I played baseball in college.
I graduated with a degree in politics and government.
I co-own a company called Claro Candles, which donates its profits to combat injustice around the world.
I have a dog named Aslan (for Narnia!).
I'm married to an amazing, beautiful, sweet woman of God: Alyssa.
I'm a dad! Kinsley Joy Bethke is my sweet little daughter.
I wrote a book (so surreal!).
I like to make creative videos.

Enough about me. I'd love to hear about you and your story as it pertains to our Bible study together. Feel free to share, critique, question, or just say hello. My contact information is below. And use #JesusIsGreater to share any thoughts with the world.

Twitter	www.twitter.com/jeffersonbethke
Instagram	www.instagram.com/jeffersonbethke
Pinterest	www.pinterest.com/jeffersonbethke
Facebook	www.facebook.com/jeffersonbethkepage
YouTube	www.youtube.com/bball1989
Blog	www.jeffbethke.com

JESUS > RELIGION

INTRODUCTION

If you've ever come across my videos, blogs, or posts, you probably know I'm quite an avid grace lover. Nothing sparks in me a joy for life and other people more than when I truly realize all God has done for me in the cross and resurrection of Jesus.

The day my life changed was when I realized that He saw all my filth, all my sin, all my shortcomings, and all my insecurities but still looked me right in the eye and said:

> I love you, and I'm not going anywhere.

That's grace. And it changes everything. The best part about being a Christian is that I don't have to have it all together, because I'm loved and pursued by a God who does. I never went searching for Him, but He went searching for me. What an awesome truth!

That's what I want to share with you through this study. The crazy journey leading up to this Bible study you're holding in your hands began with a poem I wrote for an open-mic night when I was in college. "Why I Hate Religion but Love Jesus" was the second poem I'd ever written like that, and I wanted to engage my peers with what I had experienced to be true about the person of Jesus. I wanted to acknowledge a lot of the common objections I'd heard in personal conversations—mostly related to religion. But I also wanted to encourage people not to stop with hurts and hang-ups regarding religion and to see the hope, love, and freedom of Jesus and the grace He gives so generously.

A friend of mine suggested that we shoot a video in front of a local public high school, and we put it up on YouTube, not knowing whether anyone would ever see it. We were just having fun, doing the things we enjoyed doing. But more people than we ever imagined seemed to resonate with the message. Literally millions of people have seen it, sparking thousands of conversations that I hope ultimately point people to Jesus. That video led to a book, which led to more videos, including this Bible study, and here we are now.

So for these next six sessions together, let's make a deal. I'll be honest and share the joy I've come to know in Jesus. And you take off your mask too, being honest with yourself, real with your group, and open to what Jesus wants to do in your life. Let's see where that leads. Deal?

By the way, if you'd like to hear the story behind the poem, watch the bonus video on the DVD or at *www.lifeway.com/JesusIsGreater* on your own or in your group.

WHY I HATE RELIGION BUT LOVE JESUS
Poem by Jefferson Bethke

What if I told you Jesus came to abolish religion?
What if I told you voting Republican really wasn't His mission?
What if I told you Republican doesn't automatically mean Christian,
And just because you call some people blind doesn't automatically give you vision.
I mean, if religion is so great, why has it started so many wars?
Why does it build huge churches but fail to feed the poor?
Tells single moms God doesn't love them if they've ever had a divorce,
But in the Old Testament God actually calls religious people whores.

Religion might preach grace, but another thing they practice,
Tend to ridicule God's people; they did it to John the Baptist.
They can't fix their problems, and so they just mask it,
Not realizing religion is like spraying perfume on a casket.
See, the problem with religion is that it never gets to the core.
It's just behavior modification, like a long list of chores.
Like let's dress up the outside, make it look nice and neat,
But it's funny that's what they used to do to mummies while the corpse rots underneath.

Now I ain't judging; I'm just saying quit putting on a fake look,
Because there's a problem if people only know that you're a Christian by your Facebook.
I mean, in every other aspect of life, you know that logic's unworthy.
It's like saying you play for the Lakers just because you bought a jersey.
See, this was me too, but no one seemed to be on to me,
Acting like a church kid while addicted to pornography.
See, on Sunday I'd go to church but Saturday getting faded,
As if I was simply created to have sex and get wasted.
See, I spent my whole life building this facade of neatness,
But now that I know Jesus, I boast in my weakness.

Because if grace is water, then the church should be an ocean.
It's not a museum for good people; it's a hospital for the broken.
Which means I don't have to hide my failures; I don't have to hide my sin,
Because it doesn't depend on me; it depends on Him.
See, when I was God's enemy and certainly not a fan,
He looked down and said, "I want that man!"

Which is why Jesus hated religion, and for it He called them fools.
Don't you see He's so much better than just following some rules?
Now let me clarify: I love the church, I love the Bible, and yes, I believe in sin,
But if Jesus came to your church, would they actually let Him in?
Remember, He was called a glutton and a drunkard by "religious men,"
But the Son of God never supports self-righteousness—not now, not then.

Now back to the point; one thing is vital to mention:
How Jesus and religion are on opposite spectrums.
One's the work of God, and one's a man-made invention.
One is the cure, but the other's the infection.
Because religion says do; Jesus says done.
Religion says slave; Jesus says son.
Religion puts you in bondage, but Jesus sets you free.
Religion makes you blind, but Jesus makes you see.

And that is why religion and Jesus are two different clans.
Religion is man searching for God, but Christianity is God searching for man.
Which is why salvation is freely mine, and forgiveness is my own,
Not based on my merits but Jesus' obedience alone.
Because He took the crown of thorns and the blood that dripped down His face.
He took what we all deserved; I guess that's why you call it grace.
While being murdered, He yelled, "Father, forgive them; they know not what they do."
Because when He was dangling on that cross, He was thinking of you.
He absorbed all your sin, and He buried it in the tomb.
Which is why I'm kneeling at the cross now saying, "Come on; there's room."

So for religion, know I hate it; in fact, I literally resent it.
Because when Jesus said, "It is finished," I believe He meant it.

Watch Jefferson recite this poem at *www.youtube.com/bball1989*

HOW TO USE THIS STUDY

Jesus > Religion is a six-session Bible study. Most groups meet weekly, completing one session a week, but feel free to follow a plan that meets the needs and schedule of the people in your group.

Each session of *Jesus > Religion* consists of two major sections of content, each with its own distinct features: group and personal.

1. EACH SESSION OPENS WITH GROUP CONTENT, INCLUDING:

START

This page includes questions to get the conversation started and to introduce the video segment.

WATCH

This page includes key points and Scripture references from Jefferson's teaching and space to take personal notes while watching the video.

RESPOND

This page includes questions and statements to help you and your group respond to the Bible and Jefferson's video teaching.

Everyone will be able to participate and benefit from the group content simply by showing up for each session. Think of this time together as a great starting point. Group discussion is an important step in personal growth.

Tips for leading a group can be found on the following pages (pages 10–11). Leaders are provided with valuable help to make sure everyone's time studying *Jesus > Religion* is a life-changing experience.

2. EACH SESSION OFFERS INDIVIDUAL CONTENT, INCLUDING:

PERSONAL READING

These pages are designed to help you discover what God's Word has to say about the topic you've discussed in your group session. They include selected Bible verses and questions to help you understand or apply what you're reading. This content guides you to a deeper understanding of the biblical truths presented and discussed in the group time.

The goal of this section isn't to fulfil a religious obligation and check Bible reading off your spiritual to-do list. The goal of this personal study is to help you grow in your relationship with Jesus. Personal relationships naturally include spending time with people, getting to know them, and listening to what they say. This is true with Jesus too. The more time you spend in God's Word, the better you get to know Him.

PERSONAL REFLECTION

These pages are designed to help you creatively process what you've studied. Artistic elements are used in the videos, so this is your chance to express what's on your heart and mind. Often, actions like journaling, drawing, writing lyrics, or making lists can help you sort through ideas and emotions, coming to a place of clarity about who Jesus is and your relationship with Him. So although different activities might be suggested, feel free to do whatever works best for you.

Each week includes three personal readings, each of which provides a page for personal reflection. So if you like to do something every day, complete a reading one day, then the creative reflection the next day, and so on. If you know every other day would be a good average for you to study, then complete a reading and reflection together for three days each week—whatever best fits your rhythm and personality. Remember, this isn't a rigid formula; it's all about helping you grow in your personal relationship with Jesus.

MORE FROM THE BOOK

The opening page of each "Personal Reading & Reflection" section includes a suggestion for going even deeper into the session's focus by reading related chapters in *Jesus > Religion: Why He Is So Much Better than Trying Harder, Doing More, and Being Good Enough* by Jefferson Bethke (Nelson Books, 2013, ISBN 978-1-4002-0539-4).

TIPS FOR LEADING A GROUP

PRAYERFULLY PREPARE

Prepare for each session by—

> **reviewing the weekly material and group questions ahead of time;**
> **praying for each person in the group.**

Ask the Holy Spirit to work through you and the group discussion as you point to Jesus each week through God's Word.

MINIMIZE DISTRACTIONS

Create a comfortable environment. If group members are uncomfortable, they'll be distracted and therefore not engaged in the group experience. Plan ahead by taking into consideration—

> **seating;**
> **temperature;**
> **lighting;**
> **food or drink;**
> **surrounding noise;**
> **general cleanliness (put pets away if meeting in a home).**

At best, thoughtfulness and hospitality show guests and group members they're welcome and valued in whatever environment you choose to gather. At worst, people may never notice your effort, but they're also not distracted. Do everything in your ability to help people focus on what's most important: connecting with God, with the Bible, and with others.

INCLUDE OTHERS

Your goal is to foster a community in which people are welcome just as they are but encouraged to grow spiritually. Always be aware of opportunities to—

> **invite** new people to join your group;
> **include** any people who visit the group.

An inexpensive way to make first-time guests feel welcome or to invite people to get involved is to give them their own copies of this Bible study book.

ENCOURAGE DISCUSSION

A good small group has the following characteristics.

Everyone participates. Encourage everyone to ask questions, share responses, or read aloud.

No one dominates—not even the leader. Be sure what you say takes up less than half of your time together as a group. Politely redirect discussion if anyone dominates.

Nobody is rushed through questions. Don't feel that a moment of silence is a bad thing. People often need time to think about their responses to questions they've just heard or to gain courage to share what God is stirring in their hearts.

Input is affirmed and followed up. Make sure you point out something true or helpful in a response. Don't just move on. Build personal connections with follow-up questions, asking how other people have experienced similar things or how a truth has shaped their understanding of God and the Scripture you're studying. People are less likely to speak up if they fear that you don't actually want to hear their answers or that you're looking for only a certain answer.

God and His Word are central. Opinions and experiences can be helpful, but God has given us the truth. Trust Scripture to be the authority and God's Spirit to work in people's lives. You can't change anyone, but God can. Continually point people to the Word and to active steps of faith.

KEEP CONNECTING

Think of ways to connect with group members during the week. Participation during the group session is always improved when members spend time connecting with one another away from the session. The more people are comfortable with and involved in one another's lives, the more they'll look forward to being together. When people move beyond being friendly and in the same group to truly being friends who form a community, they come to each session eager to engage instead of merely attending.

Encourage group members with thoughts, commitments, or questions from the session by connecting through—

emails;
texts;
social media.

When possible, build deeper friendships by planning or spontaneously inviting group members to join you outside your regularly scheduled group time for—

meals;
fun activities;
projects around your home, church, or community.

session one

JESUS>
RELIGION

start

WELCOME EVERYONE TO THE FIRST GROUP SESSION.
BEGIN WITH THE FOLLOWING ACTIVITIES.

If this is your first time meeting as a group or if anyone is new to the group, take a few minutes for participants to introduce themselves by answering the following questions.

When have you been surprised because something was better than you expected?

When have you missed out on something great or found yourself in an awkward situation due to a misunderstanding?

Over the next six weeks we're going to be challenged to set aside our preconceived ideas about religion and honestly consider or reconsider the person of Jesus. Keep the following question in mind as we begin this Bible study and watch the first video.

What if life with Jesus is better than you thought?

watch

USE THESE STATEMENTS TO FOLLOW ALONG AS YOU WATCH "JESUS > RELIGION."

Christianity is radically different from all other world religions.

The gospel of grace turned the world upside down.

It's not about us coming to Jesus. It's about Jesus coming to us.

Two things happen with religion.
1. You're really good at climbing the ladder, so then you're prideful.
2. You're not good at climbing the ladder, so you feel an endless cycle of despair.

Rules and institutions are beautiful when they are a response to a relationship.

There's a vast amount of encouragement when we read Scripture for what it really is, not what we want it to be.

When you let your guard down, you can be made right and transformed.

We're all looking to be known, to be loved, to have purpose. Only Jesus can give that.

SCRIPTURES: Hebrews 3:1; 4:14; 7:27; 1 Corinthians 3:16; Revelation 21:22; Psalm 32:9; Isaiah 30:16; John 1:14; 1 Peter 2:24; Ephesians 2:1; Romans 3:10-12; 4:5; 7:18-19

respond

USE THESE STATEMENTS AND QUESTIONS TO GUIDE A GROUP DISCUSSION.

Jefferson shared that he had tried religion and then walked away from it, only to realize that he had misunderstood Jesus and what being a Christian really is.

> In what way have you misunderstood Jesus or Christianity? How did you come to a better understanding?

Read Ephesians 2:4-10.

> What does this passage say about Jesus being greater than religion?

> How have you experienced being either good or bad at climbing the ladder and the resulting pride or despair?

> Have you experienced the spiritual struggle Jefferson mentioned, feeling as if you were brought to life only to become aware of your struggle with sin?

Read Romans 8:10-11.

> What hope do we have, knowing the resurrection happened and we can live in that truth?

> What other things have you put your hope and happiness in?

Read Romans 4:5.

> How does the fact that God justifies the ungodly give you freedom in this group? And in life?

> How are you encouraged to hear that the Bible is full of broken, messed-up people who were loved and changed by God's grace?

> What else did Jefferson say that was encouraging, convicting, or clarifying?

WRAP UP WITH PRAYER. ENCOURAGE EVERYONE TO COMPLETE THE PERSONAL READING & REFLECTION ON THE FOLLOWING PAGES BEFORE YOUR NEXT GROUP SESSION.

PERSONAL READING & REFLECTION

JESUS > RELIGION

We talked about a lot of things in our first group session. Maybe some ideas, interests, or questions were stirred up inside you. The topic we discussed may have even opened some old wounds, but hopefully, it gave you permission to open up your heart and mind, let down your guard, and consider whether the Jesus you've believed in (or have chosen not to believe in) is the real Jesus.

Because the real Jesus can change your life.

This week we're going to dig deeper into three ideas from the group session that will provide a foundational understanding for the rest of this study. Those three ideas are:

1. **The Bible is more than a rule book.**
2. **Christianity is more than a religion.**
3. **Jesus is more than a good man.**

Each week includes three personal readings and three pages for reflection. So if you like to study something every day, complete a reading one day, then the creative reflection the next day, and so on. If you know every other day would be a good average for you to study, then complete a reading and reflection together for three days each week. Whatever best fits your rhythm and personality.

For even more, read chapters 1–3 in the book *Jesus>Religion.*

one
MORE THAN A RULE BOOK
read

The Bible isn't filled with squeaky-clean, picture-perfect stories. The great heroes of the faith aren't all that heroic, actually. They're pretty normal. Sometimes it can even be shocking to read about their failures, rebellion, doubts, and struggles.

But that's also what's so beautiful and encouraging about the Bible. It's a grand narrative of God's grace. It's a love story and an epic battle. Jesus is the hero. Not us. The Bible describes a great rescue mission and restoration project. It shows how God is fixing everything we've broken throughout history.

If you think of the Bible as just an old book full of rules, a checklist of do's and don'ts, or a collection of inspirational stories with perfect people who achieved religious fame, you're missing out. The Bible is so much better than that.

How would you describe the Bible to someone? What is it?

Honestly, how do you feel about reading the Bible?

How often do you read it—any of it?

Does how much you read the Bible match what you say you believe about it?

Because we're going to be reading the Bible over these six weeks, let's do two things. First, let's see what the Bible says about itself. That's a good place to start, right? And then let's look at an example of a real person who expressed real feelings to a real God.

> You search the Scriptures because you think that in them
> you have eternal life; and it is they that bear witness about
> me, yet you refuse to come to me that you may have life.
> **JOHN 5:39-40**

Basically, Jesus was saying there are two ways of viewing Scripture. We can either look at it, or we can look through it. The Bible can be either a wall or a windshield. Jesus told the religious teachers of His day that it's not enough to know what the Scriptures say if we don't have a relationship with the God who says it. The Bible isn't a moral checklist to read, highlight, and memorize our way to a better life (now and eternally). The Bible is intended to help us see clearly as we follow Jesus wherever He leads us.

Circle the way you've viewed Scripture.   Wall   Windshield

Now let's look at examples of a real person who shared real feelings in a real relationship with a real God.

Read Psalm 19.

What emotions are expressed in this psalm?

How can you relate to the writer of this psalm?

Read Psalm 6.

What emotions are expressed in this psalm?

How can you relate to the writer of this psalm?

What do these psalms show you about a relationship with God?

Take time to know God. To hear His Word. To see Jesus.

reflect

Identify some favorite verses or stories from Scripture.

Creatively reflect on the fact that God wants to speak to you through the Bible. You may want to express a Scripture you identified as a prayer in your own words. You may want to draw something to remind you of an encouraging truth from God's Word. In whatever way fits your personality, use this space to express your thoughts and feelings about the truth that the Bible is much more than just a religious book of rules.

two
MORE THAN A RELIGION
read

Let's start with a few questions.

Are you a Christian?

What does that mean to you—being a Christian?

What do you think of when you hear the word *Christian?*

What perceptions do other people have of being a Christian?

You may have answered that first question the way many of us do: "Sure, of course I am. (I mean, I'm not some other religion.) I go to church. (Or I've gone some.) I have a Bible (maybe a Bible app). I try to do the right things (most of the time). I believe in God (or something). That's the box I checked on my social-media profile. (Well, technically, I checked 'other' but just because I don't like being labeled.)"

Or maybe you quickly said no. But there's something in you that's at least interested enough in Jesus to be reading this right now. Or maybe you're just at the end of your rope. Everything seems to be unraveling, so why not give religion a try? Maybe you're doing this just because somebody asked you to.

Whatever your reason or whatever you think your reason is, let's consider this question.

What if God is real? What if He's all-loving and all-powerful? What if He has a reason for your reading this right now? What if the reason is that He wants you to know Him? Do you believe you can really know God?

Remember, in the group session we defined *religion* as things we do to try to get God's approval or hopefully get into heaven when we die. And we saw that grace is the exact opposite of that mentality. Religion is trying to climb the ladder up to God. Grace is God coming down to us and giving us eternal life through what Jesus has done.

We're going to talk a lot about grace over the next six weeks. And nobody wrote more in the Bible about grace than a man named Paul, so we should look at his story.

Read Acts 9:1-19.

Wow. Maybe your story is that dramatic too, but for most of us, meeting Jesus wasn't so intense and literal. Two thousand years ago this superreligious guy named Saul (his Hebrew name), later known as Paul (his Greek name), became one of the most influential people in history. He had been such a devout Jew that he hated this new group of Jews who were claiming that Jesus was the Son of God, the promised Savior of God's people, and their true King. Paul became a religious bounty hunter of sorts, tracking down people who believed in Jesus and imprisoning them. But God had a different plan.

Read Acts 11:25-26.

The first people to be called Christians were among the first group God sent Paul to minister to. This word *Christian* wasn't originally a nice religious designation. It may have even been a derogatory term, mocking people who were living for Jesus, just as many people today are still looked down on or even persecuted for His name. The name Christian literally means *little Christ*. The idea was that these people were living as though they could know Jesus and be like Him. Their lives were so transformed by grace that they started looking more like the person of Christ than any other known religious category. This way of life didn't fit into people's preconceived boxes. This was radically different. Polar opposite.

Riots actually broke out as lives and communities were transformed. Religious leaders and even politicians felt threatened by this movement of people who were living for Jesus. Paul and the early Christians were accused of turning the world upside down (see Acts 17:6).

Look at the words Paul wrote later to a church he helped start in the city of Philippi:

> I count everything as loss because of the surpassing worth of knowing Christ Jesus my Lord. For his sake I have suffered the loss of all things and count them as rubbish, in order that I may gain Christ and be found in him, not having a righteousness of my own that comes from the law, but that which comes through faith in Christ, the righteousness from God that depends on faith.
>
> **PHILIPPIANS 3:8-9**

When it came to practicing religion, Paul had every gold star imaginable. He knew all the right answers, obeyed all the right rules, led the most elite groups, and was born into the right family (see Philippians 3:4-7). But he said compared to his relationship with Jesus, all his religious accolades were rubbish. Garbage. Dung. Worthless.

That's pretty harsh language (that would probably get him kicked out of most churches today) to say Jesus is greater than religion.

What about you? What has defined your life?

How has religious activity defined your relationship with God?

How does trying to keep the rules and look the part make you feel?

Let's go back to the first question. Are you a Christian? Whether you've said yes or no to a religious activity that's being called Christian, Jesus is greater than that.

For two thousand years women and men like Paul have faithfully lived and died and passed along the life-changing truth of Jesus. Today, right now, you have the opportunity to join that story. Are you ready to know and live for this Jesus? The Jesus who transforms lives? The Jesus who turns the world upside down through His people?

Christianity is a relationship with Jesus by grace, not effort.

reflect

Have you been trying to climb up to God through religion when He's already come down to you in Jesus? Use this space to reflect on what it means to be a Christian. You may want to draw a ladder and add things you've tried to do to be good enough for God (and others). How is a relationship with Jesus so much more than a religion?

three
MORE THAN A GOOD MAN
read

There's a certain Bible verse that's almost become a cliché. We see it all over the place. You know, the guy waving the sign during the big event. But when a popular college athlete has it written on his eye black, millions of people Google it to find out what it says, because they recognize only the numbers. People see it everywhere but don't know what it means. It's John 3:16.

> God so loved the world, that he gave his only Son, that whoever believes in him should not perish but have eternal life.
> **JOHN 3:16**

Love. Life. God's only Son. Given for whoever believes.

This story is too good to read just this one popular verse.

Read John 3:1-21.

Now there's a lot going on in this story, but here are a few things we need to notice.

1. Nicodemus was a Pharisee, meaning he was a religious leader.

2. Nicodemus came at night to meet with Jesus. The fact that this detail is included in the story suggests that nighttime wasn't just when he happened to be available to stop by. Most likely, Nicodemus didn't want his religious friends to see him asking Jesus questions. Also, by the end of the story, Jesus used light and dark to represent being in or out of relationship with God.

3. Nicodemus didn't understand what Jesus was talking about because it didn't fit into his mental framework for relating to God.

How has your understanding of Jesus changed over time?

Nicodemus called Jesus Rabbi and said, "We know that you are a teacher come from God" (v. 2). But Nicodemus's words show that he didn't know who Jesus really was.

Who do you say Jesus is? Write a simple explanation.

How would you explain the difference between respecting Jesus as a good Teacher and believing in Him?

What are some popular opinions about Jesus today?

Ultimately, what Jesus told Nicodemus is true for "whoever" (verse 16) will believe today. There's no middle ground. No respectful nod. No celebrity acceptance speech thanking God for His blessings. Jesus said we either believe in Him for salvation and live in relationship with Him or we don't.

In each pair of words or phrases, underline the choice that applies to you.

Light, dark

In relationship, out of relationship

Eternal life, perishing

Believing in Jesus, not so sure yet

Born into God's spiritual family, living for this physical world

Jesus came so that you could have life. Jesus came because of God's love.

But Jesus didn't come to get rid of everything we might associate with religion. He came to put everything back in its right place. Things were all mixed up and out of order. Just as they often are today.

God is clear throughout Scripture that what He desires, what really pleases Him, what He considers religion is something very different from what we've twisted it into. Jesus told the religious leaders:

> Go and learn what this means, "I desire mercy, and not sacrifice." For I came not to call the righteous, but sinners.
> **MATTHEW 9:13**

In your own words, explain what Jesus was saying in this verse.

Read Matthew 5:17-20.

Basically, Jesus said unless you're better at keeping all the rules than Pharisees like Nicodemus (the varsity squad, the A-Team, the religious elite), then your religion will never earn your way into heaven.

In other words, none of us are climbing that ladder and reaching the top.

Religion says do. Jesus says done.

But He *didn't* say that what's written in the Scriptures isn't true. Every bit of it is true.

We just often miss the point.

Jesus is the perfect bull's-eye.

It's all about Jesus.

reflect

Use this space to express your thoughts and feelings about the person of Jesus. Write a prayer, poetry, or song lyrics. Record questions. Draw a picture. Whatever you want to do to reflect on the truth about Jesus.

session two

LOVE
> SELF

start

WELCOME EVERYONE. START BY REVIEWING SESSION 1 BEFORE INTRODUCING SESSION 2.

Session 1 focused on the Bible, Christianity, and Jesus.

What was most helpful, encouraging, or challenging from your personal reading and reflection in session 1?

Today we'll shift our focus to relationships and comparison.

Start this session with a simple activity. Have everyone line up side by side as far away from an opposite wall as possible. Then instruct everyone to jump to the distant wall.

Who jumped the farthest distance? Shortest? Average?

It's human nature to constantly make comparisons. Keep the following question in mind as we watch the next video.

Do you look to Jesus or to people when measuring your worth?

watch

USE THESE STATEMENTS TO FOLLOW ALONG AS YOU WATCH "LOVE > SELF."

Grace and Jesus want to make friends and break down barriers. Religion puts up barriers.

With religion the spotlight is on you, and it's about comparing. But when it's about grace, the spotlight is on Jesus, and we realize we're all on an equal playing field.

When you make something other than Jesus central, that's idolatry.

Whenever you idolize something, you demonize the opposite.

Sin is the enemy.

Sin put us and God in separation from each other.

God has rescued us in the person and work of Jesus.

When you trust in grace, you are one with God.

God doesn't grade on a curve; He grades on a cross.

Comparison is an endless cycle.

When you're plugged in to God's love, you'll in turn go and love others.

SCRIPTURES: John 4:1-42; Ephesians 6:12; Colossians 1:21; Romans 5:10; 2 Corinthians 5:21; Hebrews 4:15; Matthew 22:36-40

Video sessions available at
www.lifeway.com/JesusIsGreater

respond

USE THESE STATEMENTS AND QUESTIONS TO GUIDE A GROUP DISCUSSION.

Let's start with the questions Jefferson asked at the end of the video.

What hope exists in knowing Jesus doesn't go around you, He's not afraid of your sin, and He comes to you right where you are?

How have you received God's grace? How have you shared it with others?

Explain what Jefferson meant when he said, "God doesn't grade on a curve; He grades on a cross."

How have you experienced the cycle of disappointment that results from comparing yourself to others?

Read John 4:7-10,15-18,27-30.

What seems too bad for Jesus to change in your life or in the lives of other people?

How have you seen people make enemies or demonize the opposite of what they idolize? Whom do you avoid or look down on?

Read Romans 5:10; 2 Corinthians 5:21; and Colossians 1:21-22.

How does remembering Jesus' overwhelming and sacrificial love change the way you view and treat others?

Read Matthew 22:36-40.

What practical steps can you take this week to follow Jesus' teaching to love God and love others?

WRAP UP WITH PRAYER. ENCOURAGE EVERYONE TO COMPLETE THE PERSONAL READING & REFLECTION ON THE FOLLOWING PAGES BEFORE YOUR NEXT GROUP SESSION.

PERSONAL READING & REFLECTION

LOVE >SELF

When you learn to see yourself and others through the eyes of Jesus, your life will be radically changed. He loves you. Don't just skip over that. *You. Are. Loved.*

God doesn't love the person you wish you were or the person you pretend to be. He loves you. The real you.

How freeing is that?

I don't know about you, but I've spent a lot of my life comparing myself to others, hoping I could be good enough. I'm guessing I'm not the only one and you can relate. But seeking identity and worth in anything other than Jesus is a never-ending cycle of disappointment. Our identity and worth are found only in Him.

To wrap our hearts and minds around just how explosive and powerful this truth is, we're going to look at three ideas:

1. **Grace is more than we deserve.**
2. **Humility means thinking of yourself less.**
3. **Love is the greatest commandment.**

For even more, read chapters 4–5 in the book *Jesus>Religion.*

one
MORE THAN WE DESERVE
read

Grace is scandalous.

It's more than we deserve. In fact, grace is getting something we don't deserve at all. It's a good gift we could never earn (see Romans 11:6). When we introduced grace last week, we learned that it's the opposite of religion—the opposite of trying harder to do the right things to deserve God's favor. Today we're going to look even more closely at grace. Let's move beyond the concept and see how grace transforms our lives.

Read John 4:1-6.

Religion makes enemies. Jesus makes friends. He doesn't go around us. He comes straight to us. Recall in the group session we learned that Jews and Samaritans were bitter rivals. They hated each other. The root of this disdain and prejudice was religious. Jews viewed Samaritans as people who had compromised the purity of the Jewish religion by integrating into a foreign culture. But instead of dismissing and avoiding people, Jesus *had* to go to them (see verse 4). His mission and purpose on this earth were to extend God's love and grace to whoever would believe in Him (see John 3:16.)

Whom do you avoid? Why?

How would you feel if God wanted to change their lives? Would you celebrate the change, or would you question God? Does your response suggest that you believe you deserve God's love and grace more than these people do?

Read John 4:7-15.

The woman immediately questioned Jesus from a cultural and religious perspective. We can't read her tone of voice, so we don't know whether her questions were bitter or sincere. But we know she had baggage and Jesus wasn't deterred by her questions. He put the religious and cultural differences aside and got personal.

Read John 4:16-30.

Notice that when Jesus got personal, the woman turned the conversation into a religious debate. But Jesus is greater than religion. He kept the conversation focused on her need for love and grace. He offered her the very thing she had presumably been seeking in relationships with men. The living water Jesus offers is eternally satisfying.

> **Where are you seeking satisfaction and relief? What have you tried to fill your life with? What wells are you going to? What relationships are you using or being used by?**

> **What religious questions have you heard or used as reasons for not making a decision about Jesus?**

Jesus was talking to a Samaritan (strike 1), a woman (strike 2) with a past littered from the wreckage of broken relationships and probably currently living in sexual sin (strike 3 — she should be out). There was no way Jesus should be anywhere near this woman from a cultural and religious perspective. This was as scandalous as it could get. But Jesus came to her and showed her grace.

Read John 4:39-42.

After experiencing the unconditional, nonjudgmental, free grace of Jesus, the woman dropped everything and ran to tell others.

> **When did you first personally experience the grace of Jesus, or have you only heard others talk about it?**

> **Whom do you know who needs to experience the grace of Jesus for themselves?**

Jesus doesn't avoid you. He comes to give you grace.

reflect

Think about the loneliness of the woman at the well. A culture that didn't value her. A string of relationships with no commitment. And alone drawing water in the middle of the day. That's significant. In cultures where water was drawn from wells outside town, women typically walked together for safety and company in the morning or evening when it was cooler. It can be assumed this woman was an outsider even in regard to her own culture. Because of her history with men, maybe she had earned a reputation worthy of glances, harsh words, or the silent treatment from other women. She was doing hard work in the hottest part of the day. Alone. But Jesus *had* to be there waiting. Full of grace.

Reflect on the fact that Jesus meets you, knows everything about you—even the stuff you're most ashamed of—and offers grace.

two
THINKING OF YOURSELF LESS
read

Love, by nature, is an act of humility. In our culture humility is sometimes misunderstood. Some people think to be humble is a sign of weakness or means letting people walk all over us. But from a biblical perspective, humility isn't about putting ourselves down but about lifting others up.

True humility is not thinking less of yourself; it is thinking of yourself less.[1]

Explain this idea in your own words. How does this quotation help you understand humility?

We've already established that religion is focused on you. It's about what you need to do right. This effort to perform naturally leads to pride for getting things right or to self-loathing for getting things wrong. Both of these miss the bull's-eyes of godly humility and the Christian life, which are focused on Jesus.

Read Romans 12:3.

Explain this verse in your own words. What does it say about humility?

What you read about humility and grace came immediately after Paul's encouragement to Roman Christ followers not to be "conformed to this world, but be transformed by the renewal of your mind" (see Romans 12:2). And it came immediately before a metaphor describing Christians as individual parts of the same body—each different but equally valuable (see Romans 12:4-5). The common factor in both of these popular passages of Scripture is a humble attitude.

Read Romans 12:4-5.

How does Paul's teaching about valuing personal differences and working together for the sake of a common purpose add to your understanding of Christlike humility?

When your identity and worth are found in your relationship with Jesus, you're freed from the endless cycle of comparing yourself to others. You don't have to one-up and outdo anybody. People are no longer competition when you aren't living to prove yourself to anyone else. You're living to please God.

Read Romans 12:2.

According to this verse, how can you break free from a worldly perspective?

When Paul wrote that we can know the good, acceptable, and perfect will of God, he implied that our natural way of thinking and living without Him isn't good, acceptable, or perfect. The pattern of this world is a never-ending cycle of comparison and despair. Even so-called religious activity, when focused on ourselves instead of on Jesus, is vain and meaningless.

Read Ephesians 2:8-9.

How do these verses absolutely destroy religious effort, pride, and comparison to others?

According to Ephesians 2:8-9, explain how a relationship with Jesus and an understanding of grace make pride impossible.

The truth is that you're loved and accepted by God's grace alone—not by your works—so you have nothing to boast about. That doesn't mean you won't still be tempted to compare yourself to others. You may be tempted to feel you're better than people who don't yet know Jesus or those who know Him but aren't as good at doing the right things as you are. But Jesus leaves no room for pride and comparison. Everyone needs His love and grace.

Read John 8:1-11.

This is another story in John's Gospel about the beautiful and scandalous grace of Jesus. Surrounded by religious leaders puffed up with moral pride, this woman was literally being looked down on. Imagine the humiliation and fear she must have experienced when she was dragged into public for judgment and execution. Yes, this woman was guilty of sin according to the law, but adultery requires two guilty persons (see Leviticus 20:10; Deuteronomy 22:22). Where was the man? And how did these Pharisees catch her in the act?

Besides the obvious pride, there were all kinds of awful things going on here. Put yourself in this scene. One moment this woman was involved in the act of adultery, the next she was seized by religious leaders and forced into public, and then she was lying at the feet of Jesus. Let that shock and shame sink in. Feel the crushing weight of the religious leaders' pride and arrogance—the hateful self-righteousness that so desperately wanted to be right that it was willing to throw rocks at this woman … until she died … in front of Jesus.

How did Jesus respond to the Pharisees?

How did Jesus respond to the woman?

What do Jesus' responses reveal about pride and humility?

Don't think too much of yourself or too little of others. We all need God's grace.

reflect

How you are like—

the woman in John 8:1-11?

the Pharisees in John 8:1-11?

1. Rick Warren, *The Purpose-Driven Life* (Grand Rapids: Zondervan, 2002), 148.

three
THE GREATEST COMMANDMENTS
read

Jesus was so radically different from anyone who had ever lived that people weren't sure what to do with Him. Jesus didn't fit into anybody's box.

Religious leaders were constantly challenging Jesus. They wanted to prove they were right and to trap Him into saying or doing something wrong. There were two primary religious groups in Scripture who had a competitive attitude toward Jesus. Viewing Him as a threat to their status and influence among the people, they treated Jesus like an opponent to defeat and eventually as an enemy to kill (see John 11:45-53).

1. The Sadducees, the priestly class who ran the temple, were generally highly educated and wealthy. Their privileged religious box didn't have room for beliefs like the resurrection of the dead. Pride kept them from what they couldn't explain or control.

2. The Pharisees were fundamentalists and legalists; they loved being better than everyone. Their strict moral boxes were full of rules, traditions, and hard work. Pride made them constantly obsess over every detail in their pursuit of perfection.

Ironically, both groups seemed to believe they had God on their side. They were devoted to God but oppressive and condescending toward people. One thing they agreed on enough to stop competing against each other was uniting their efforts against Jesus. He completely blew up both of their boxes with revolutionary love, unflinching truth, and scandalous grace.

Read Matthew 22:34-40.

The Sadducees' attempt to outsmart Jesus and publicly embarrass Him backfired miserably, so the Pharisees called in an expert. The question the lawyer asked Jesus wasn't sincere. It was a political trap to get Jesus to take sides for or against popular schools of thought, therefore discrediting Him as a Teacher of the law. But again, this tactic backfired when Jesus provided an irrefutable summary of the entire law.

What did Jesus say are the two greatest commandments?

What do the two commands have in common?

Is one of these easier for you to obey? If so, which one? Why do you think it's easier?

By answering with two commands, Jesus showed where religious pride stops short. It's not enough to do what we think proves our love for God if we don't also have love for people. So our natural response is then to narrowly define exactly whom we have to love.

Read Luke 10:29-37.

According to Jesus' response, how would you answer the question, Who is my neighbor?

What does it mean to love your neighbor?

Why was it shocking that the hero of the story was a Samaritan, not someone with a religious job (the priest) or a religious family (the Levite)?

Read Matthew 5:38-48.

In case it isn't clear yet just how scandalous the grace of Jesus is, He removes any doubt about exactly whom we should love. If your love isn't radically humble, then Jesus asks how you are any different from someone who hasn't experienced life-changing grace in the family of God. God's love is bigger than you. It's meant to be shared with the people around you—people you like and people you don't.

How is humility at the heart of the kind of love Jesus described?

Paul described the revolutionary love of Jesus this way:

> Now in Christ Jesus you who once were far off have been brought near by the blood of Christ. For he himself is our peace, who has made us both one and has broken down in his flesh the dividing wall of hostility.
> **EPHESIANS 2:13-14**

The temple where Jesus walked and taught had several courts divided by walls and curtains. Certain categories of people were permitted into only particular courts. Gentiles (non-Jewish people), women, Jewish men, the priestly class, and the high priest each had varied degrees of access to the different areas. And only one person, the high priest, could enter the innermost part, the holy of holies, at a particular time of year after performing certain rituals. When Jesus died on the cross for our sins, that curtain, dividing the most holy place between God and man, tore from top to bottom, as if the hands of God had ripped it in half (see Mark 15:38). No more division. Only love, grace, and mercy.

Religion puts up walls. Religion draws lines. Religion makes enemies. It leads to an endless cycle of comparison. Ultimately, it leads to pride, which is the heart of sin. Pride separates. Sin puts us in conflict with God and with people.

Jesus was tearing down barriers and bridging the gaps, bringing people together. He was removing sin and its consequences. And making a new life possible. Unlike the religious leaders, who were known for their status, traditions, and morality, Jesus said His disciples would live by a renewed understanding of the commandments:

> A new commandment I give to you, that you love one another: just as I have loved you, you also are to love one another. By this all people will know that you are my disciples, if you have love for one another."
> **JOHN 13:34-35**

When people look at you, do they see Jesus?

Love God. Love people. All of them. There's nothing greater.

reflect

Be specific. What does it look like for you to—

"love the Lord your God with all your heart and with all your soul and with all your mind" (Matthew 22:37)?

"love your neighbor as yourself" (Matthew 22:39)?

session three

GIVER
>GIFTS

start

WELCOME EVERYONE AND START BY REVIEWING SESSION 2 BEFORE INTRODUCING SESSION 3.

Session 2 focused on grace, humility, and love.

What was most helpful, encouraging, or challenging from your personal reading and reflection in session 2?

Today we'll shift our focus to blessings and joy.

What's the greatest gift you ever received and why?

Sometimes we value something in and of itself. Other times—and most often with gifts—the value of something is enhanced by the relationship of the person who gave it to us or by the history behind it. Keep the following question in mind as we watch the next video.

Do you love Jesus for who He is or for what you hope to get from Him?

watch

USE THESE STATEMENTS TO FOLLOW ALONG AS YOU WATCH "GIVER > GIFTS."

What if following Jesus isn't about getting stuff?

Worshiping Jesus is what life is all about.

No matter what, Jesus is the one thing that can't be taken.

The base sin in our lives is idolatry.

Anything other than Jesus is an idol.

God is saying these things about idolatry because He wants to give us the most joy possible.

He's the Creator, so He knows how to bring us the most joy possible.

Suffering can be used to take our hands off things that can be broken and put them on God.

When your hope and identity are in the Creator, true joy is found.

SCRIPTURES: Romans 1:25; 8:35-39; James 1:17; Exodus 20:1-17; John 10:10; 15:11; Matthew 6:19-21; Hebrews 6:17-20; 12:28; Ephesians 1:3

Video sessions available at
www.lifeway.com/JesusIsGreater

respond

USE THESE STATEMENTS AND QUESTIONS TO GUIDE A GROUP DISCUSSION.

Let's start with some questions Jefferson asked in the video.

If everything in your life were taken away, would Jesus be enough?

What would cause the most damage if it were taken from you?

When have you tried to use God to get things you wanted?

Read Matthew 6:19-21.

What does Jesus teach about the source of our hope and happiness?

Read Romans 8:35-39.

What encouragement do these verses and the story of Dmitri provide about the love of Jesus and your circumstances?

Read James 1:17.

When do you most often focus on gifts instead of the Giver?

How can you focus on the Giver instead of just gifts?

Read John 10:10; 15:11.

What does Jesus want to give us?

In your own words, how would you answer the question Jefferson asked in the video: What's the point of following Jesus?

WRAP UP WITH PRAYER. ENCOURAGE EVERYONE TO COMPLETE THE PERSONAL READING & REFLECTION ON THE FOLLOWING PAGES BEFORE YOUR NEXT GROUP SESSION.

PERSONAL READING & REFLECTION

GIVER >GIFTS

Another form of comparison and self-focus is to believe that if God is good and really loves us, He will bless us with more things. But health, wealth, and success aren't proof of God's favor or of a right relationship with Him. Too often our attention is laser-focused on being blessed instead of being loved and counting our many blessings. To desire God's gifts more than the Giver Himself is idolatry and will never satisfy us.

Jesus is more satisfying than anything in this world. To know and trust Jesus gives rest and joy greater than any circumstance, good or bad. And anyone who has lived more than a few moments in this world knows that life will sometimes be hard. While God doesn't delight in suffering, He uses seasons of rain to bring about growth and beauty. Our hope and satisfaction are ultimately found in the spiritual reality of God's love for us in Jesus and the promise that all things will be made right. Ultimately, there will be resurrection, justice, and healing. Jesus is enough. He's better than good things. He's better than bad times.

We'll keep three things in mind as we focus on being fully satisfied in Jesus:

1. **Idolatry is simply too much of a good thing.**
2. **He's the Giver of every good and perfect gift.**
3. **There's more to life than this world.**

For even more, read chapters 6–7 in the book *Jesus>Religion.*

one
TOO MUCH OF A GOOD THING
read

Do you ever view God like Santa Claus?

I don't mean imagining Him with a white beard and living far away in a magical, happy place on top of the world, although that description fits a lot of popular misunderstandings about God. What I mean is, have you ever acted as if God exists just to give you what you want as long as you're good enough to deserve it? And Santa grades on a pretty easy curve when it comes to naughty and nice, right? So as long as we're not awful compared to other people, we should get what we want.

This is how I used to view God at times. If I was at least as good as everyone else, I expected to have a pretty good life and to get into heaven when I died. Based on what I did, I expected to get what I wanted in return.

Basically, this is using God, not loving Him.

It's treating God like a vending machine. You're putting something into your relationship with God only in order to get something out of it. It's all about you and what you want. But God isn't a genie in a bottle to grant your wishes and make your dreams come true.

To put this in biblical terms, we're talking about idolatry.

That might sound pretty harsh and foreign, right? After all, you probably don't worship statues made of wood, stone, or precious metals. But in Colossians 3:5 Paul explained that covetousness is idolatry.

Covetousness is a biblical term we don't use too much today. It's basically like greed and jealousy rolled into one desire. To covet is to want something that somebody else has—and maybe even believe you deserve at least as much as, if not more than, they do. Covetousness is an insatiable hunger that eats away at you. No matter what you get, you'll never be satisfied.

What or whom have you felt that you had to have?

Did you get what you wanted? If so, how long were you satisfied?

Read Exodus 20:3-4; Romans 1:21-25.

What do these verses reveal about idolatry?

Worship is another word you probably associate with religion. But in its simplest essence it means making something the ultimate object of your affection—a relationship, an activity, an achievement, a possession, or an experience. Whatever motivates your decisions, influences your lifestyle, consumes your thoughts, and excites your passion is an object of worship.

Who or what is most important in your life? (Consider this question honestly. Don't write what you want the answer to be or think it should be, but look at your life and identify what you love most. Nobody else has to see your answer.)

The trickiest thing about idolatry in our culture today is that many times it doesn't appear evil. We probably don't bow and pray to images of animals or deities, but all our hearts are bent toward idolizing what we can see and living for what we can get.

Often idolatry takes the form of turning something good into our god. It's putting the created thing in the place of our Creator (see Romans 1:25). Idolatry is an unhealthy and disproportionate amount of affection we've placed on anything other than God. Too much of a good thing becomes a really bad thing.

God isn't a vending machine, a genie in a bottle, or a cosmic Santa Claus to be used for what we can get from Him. He alone is worthy of our worship. He's the One who created us and the things we're tempted to love more than Him. He alone can satisfy us. He alone can truly love us in return and give us what we need, even if it isn't always what we want.

No created thing is greater than the One who created it.

reflect

Use this page to express your worship—your love and devotion—to God. Keep in mind that He created you and everything in this world. Ask Him to show you ways you've been living for other things—lesser things.

two
EVERY GOOD & PERFECT GIFT
read

A better way to view God than Santa Claus is Father. This is a common description of God in the Bible and the term Jesus used often.

What do you think of when you hear the word *Father?*

Whether you have a positive, negative, or mixed reaction to the word *Father,* based on your personal experiences, you can be sure God is the perfect Father. He's what a father should be.

Any positive experiences you have with earthly fathers point you toward an even greater Heavenly Father. Good fathers give us a small picture of what a relationship with God can be. But no earthly father is perfect.

Any negative experience you may have had with a father—even the absence of a father—is painful because you know what a father is supposed to be. You know that relationship is supposed to be safe, supportive, and characterized by unconditional love.

One part of our relationship with God that we distort and make unhealthy is a misplaced affection for the things He gives us.

Read James 1:17.

How is God described in this verse?

How are you comforted or encouraged by the image of light that James used to describe God's character?

What does James 1:17 say about God's gifts?

We've already seen that it's human nature to become obsessed with the gifts God gives us. We turn good things into our gods and worship them, giving them our affection and allowing them to consume our lives.

Earlier James warned people that temptation and sin don't come from God but from within our own hearts when we desire things instead of God. It's true that gifts are from God (see James 1:13-16). But the Giver is much greater than the gifts He gives us.

When have you blamed God for temptation or sin in your life?

What temptations feel the hardest to resist?

What empty promise does this temptation make, proving to be an idol with no real power to give you what you desire?

You can identify what you idolize by recognizing what tempts you. If something is enticing, part of you believes it's more satisfying and pleasing than what God can give you. Whatever lures your heart away from loving your Heavenly Father is an idol. Anything that has your devotion and influences your life more than Jesus is an idol, a distortion of the good and perfect gifts the Father gives.

Read Ephesians 1:3.

Paul wrote this letter to the Christians in a city called Ephesus, a center of idolatry. Ephesus was the home of the temple of Artemis, one of the most popular Greek goddesses, the daughter of Zeus and the twin sister of Apollo. She was a seriously big deal in ancient religion. Her temple was not only one of the seven wonders of the ancient world but was also deemed as the most magnificent. At one point the craftsmen and merchants who made a lot of money selling shrines of Artemis stirred up a riot after Paul preached the gospel of Jesus (see Acts 19:24-41). People in the city had been transformed by the love and grace of Jesus, and they were worshiping Jesus instead of Artemis and "the sacred stone that fell from the sky" (verse 35).

Why is Paul's description of Jesus in Ephesians 1:3 so significant and revolutionary for the people of Ephesus?

Why is it still significant to know that you've been blessed in Christ "with every spiritual blessing in the heavenly places"?

Paul said everything you need is found in your relationship with Jesus. He's infinitely greater than anything in this world. He wants to bless you. He wants you to experience life to its fullest. He's not a cosmic killjoy who wants to ruin all your fun. He has the very best intentions for you. And the things you think you want apart from Him aren't good. Jesus said:

> The thief comes only to steal and kill and destroy. I came that they may have life and have it abundantly.
> **JOHN 10:10**

In your own words, what is Jesus' desire for your life?

Read Matthew 7:7-11.

No matter what your experiences are with fathers in this world, Jesus said you can trust your Heavenly Father. He's always good. He not only knows what you need but also wants to bless you with good gifts.

What are you worried about, fearing that God won't give you what you need? Do you worry that God will give you bad things?

Your Heavenly Father loves you. You have everything you'll ever need through your relationship with His Son, Jesus. Don't be afraid to ask in prayer. God gives only what's good.

God's gifts are good. Enjoy them. But the Giver is even better. Enjoy Him more.

reflect

Every good thing in your life is a gift from God. Take time to identify as many good things in your life as possible. Let your gratitude move beyond those good things to the even greater God who gave them to you.

three
MORE THAN THIS WORLD
read

If God is a good Father who gives good gifts, why is life so bad at times? You don't have to watch the news or scroll through social media long to see what a mess the world is in.

What examples of brokenness do you see in this world?

A major problem with the Santa Claus image of God is that you have to conclude when life is hard that you somehow deserve bad things. The other alternatives are that He must be either cruel with His power or powerless to do anything to help you in your distress.

But if the Bible is to be trusted—and I believe it is—then God is a good, loving, and all-powerful Father. This world is broken because of sin, the prideful root of all conflict between God and other people. But God is at work through Jesus to restore it all.

Read Revelation 21:1-5.

What hope is expressed in these verses?

What specific areas of your life need the hope that all things will be made new?

Until that time what do you do when life hurts? What should you do when you want to scream or cry or shout to God, "Why?" Do it. Be honest. Let your cries drive you closer to God as you recognize your desperate need for His strength.

Personally, what I really want isn't an answer for why pain and suffering exist. What I really want is for God to fix it. What I really need is to know He's still with me and has everything under control even if it doesn't look like it from my perspective.

The truth is, in Jesus, God has begun fixing everything and will ultimately renew all creation.

And before we start to feel that God is a distant, impersonal Deity who can't understand or doesn't care that life is hard, remember that He came, lived among us, and let the people He created and came to save kill Him by nailing Him to a cross. Jesus knows what you're going through. He's lived, suffered, and died. He's been hungry, tired, betrayed, rejected, beaten, and murdered.

But there's hope.

Because He rose again, and He's alive with all power and authority in heaven and on earth.

Our hope and satisfaction are in God's love for us in Jesus and the promise that all things will be made right:

> I have said these things to you, that in me you may
> have peace. In the world you will have tribulation.
> But take heart; I have overcome the world.
> **JOHN 16:33**

Honestly ask yourself if you got everything you wanted but didn't have Jesus, would you be content?

If you had only Jesus, would you have peace despite your circumstances?

Read Mark 10:17-27.

This is another story of someone who approached Jesus with a question. This time the young man seemed sincere with his question, but Jesus' response still wasn't what he expected or wanted.

What did the young man's action reveal about his source of hope, security, worth, and identity?

Sometimes people say, "Don't ever say you won't do something, or that's exactly what God will want you to do." What a tragic misunderstanding of God's heart. Jesus wasn't bullying this young man. He loved him. Remember, Jesus came to give abundant life (see John 10:10), and God is the Giver of all good and perfect gifts (see James 1:17).

Is there anything in this world worth more than Jesus?

What would you have the hardest time trusting Jesus with?

What does the humorous image of a camel and needle have to do with grace (see Mark 10:25)?

Read Matthew 6:19-34.

Jesus addressed several things we idolize or worry about. Which is most challenging for you?

Jesus said days will have trouble and things in this world will fall apart (see John 16:33). What hope did He offer?

Jesus is enough. He's our hope.

Better than good things. Better than bad times.

reflect

Cry out to God. Express your broken heart in total transparency. Praise Him that He will make all things new and until that time, Jesus is enough. He's your anchor of hope (see Hebrews 6:19).

session four

COVENANT
>CONTRACT

start

WELCOME EVERYONE AND START BY REVIEWING SESSION 3 BEFORE INTRODUCING SESSION 4.

Session 4 focused on idolatry, God as Father, and hope.

What was most helpful, encouraging, or challenging from your personal reading and reflection in session 3?

Today we'll take an even deeper look at our relationship with God through Christ.

What's the most meaningful promise anyone has ever kept to you?

What's the worst experience you've ever had with a broken commitment?

Relationships are built on trust. We know everyone is imperfect; we'll let others down, and others will let us down. But Jesus is perfectly faithful. Keep the following question in mind as we watch the next video.

What does a relationship with Jesus look like?

watch

USE THESE STATEMENTS TO FOLLOW ALONG AS YOU WATCH "COVENANT > CONTRACT."

Insanity is doing the same thing and expecting different results.

Scripture says God is looking for us.

A covenant is about the promise, not the behavior.

A contract is about the behavior, not a promise.

God is a Father.

To be a Christian is about identity, not activity. Activity flows from that identity.

Joy comes from understanding covenant first, and behavior comes from that.

Coming to Jesus is the beginning of the road, not the end.

You have freedom to take off the mask when you're in covenant love.

You are a child of the living God—under covenant, not contract.

SCRIPTURES: Luke 15:1-2,11-32; Matthew 23:23; Romans 1:25; Deuteronomy 7:9; Genesis 3:8-9

respond

USE THESE STATEMENTS AND QUESTIONS TO GUIDE A GROUP DISCUSSION.

In the depths of your soul, do you believe you're a child of God? Or do you live like an employee who hopes not to upset the boss?

When have you felt you're one sin from God's giving up on you?

Read Luke 15:1-2.

What encouragement or conviction does it give you to know that Jesus reached out to sinners and that they were attracted to Him?

Read Luke 15:11-32.

Are you more like the rebellious or entitled son in this story? In what ways?

When have you experienced the grace of the Heavenly Father?

How does understanding that you're a child under covenant, not under contract, change your view of God?

How does it change your view of sin and forgiveness to know that your Father celebrates your return?

Jefferson explained that the gospel isn't just for saving you, and then you try to live a better life so that God won't be mad. The gospel is relevant every day, especially when you mess up.

Identify ways you need Jesus each day.

Read Genesis 3:8-9.

What was man's response to sin? God's response?

Starting right now, how can you come out of hiding, take off your mask, and experience the joy and freedom of Christ?

WRAP UP WITH PRAYER. ENCOURAGE EVERYONE TO COMPLETE THE PERSONAL READING & REFLECTION ON THE FOLLOWING PAGES BEFORE YOUR NEXT GROUP SESSION.

PERSONAL READING & REFLECTION

COVENANT > CONTRACT

Grace is scandalous. The fact that God loves the ungodly is unthinkable. But the fact that Jesus was a friend of sinners and was rejected by the religious is undeniable. Throughout scriptural history as well as today, people can't free themselves from sin. Salvation comes only by the grace of God through the blood of His Son, Jesus. No amount of moral conduct or religious ritual will ever earn abundant life in this world or eternity with God. We can be free from the slavery of our own efforts to bring satisfaction to our lives. In Christ there's no condemnation, no shame, no hiding, no mask. We're free to truly experience the love and grace of God and His people.

Truly grasping the freeing power of God's grace helps us realize the following truths.

1. **Freedom is better than faking it.**
2. **Family is more than just a name.**
3. **Failure doesn't equal firing.**

For even more, read chapter 8 in the book *Jesus>Religion.*

one
FREEDOM IS BETTER THAN FAKING IT
read

Freedom. We're not talking red, white, and blue democracy. Being a Christian isn't about being a Republican, a Democrat, or even an American. While we can be grateful for political liberties in our country, an even greater freedom exists no matter where we live.

Freedom isn't the license to do whatever you want. That's slavery to your own self-centered desires—also known as sin. Jesus set you free from the ruthless master of your desires. That life wasn't working out too well. Turns out sin is a cruel master that always pays with death (see Romans 6:15-23). That's not life at all. It's definitely not freedom.

Freedom also isn't about flaunting your liberty, proving to others that although you're a Christian, you aren't legalistic. Ironically, that's slavery to your so-called freedom.

Read Galatians 5:13-14.

When have you twisted freedom into a license to do whatever you wanted?

How does freedom give you an opportunity to focus on others instead of on yourself?

Jesus didn't pay the price for our sin just to have us become slaves to self-effort:

> For freedom Christ has set us free; stand firm therefore,
> and do not submit again to a yoke of slavery.
> **GALATIANS 5:1**

That first part sounds obvious, right? But Scripture is clear—and so are our personal experiences—that our natural tendency is toward religion. Toward effort. Control. Slavery. That's the very definition of *insanity:* doing the same thing over and over but expecting different results. Our efforts couldn't save us. We could never earn God's approval through religion. We were set free from effort, illusions of control, and the slavery of religion, but we keep going back to the idea that we have to try harder and be good enough. Even if we believe we were saved by grace alone through faith, not works, we somehow buy into the lie that our relationship with Jesus is now up to us. Paul put it this way:

Are you so foolish? Having begun by the Spirit,
are you now being perfected by the flesh?
GALATIANS 3:3

In what specific areas do you slip back into believing your relationship with God relies entirely on what you do?

In what way is that belief slavery instead of freedom?

Freedom is embracing the truth, not keeping it at a distance. God justifies the ungodly (see Romans 5:6). You don't have to pretend to be perfect. You need Jesus. Every day. You need His grace today just as much as you did when you first trusted Him to give you a new life and identity. Stop faking it. Take off your mask. Run to Him.

Read Genesis 3:1-13.

It's natural to hide and blame. The very first people on earth hid and then tried to pass the blame for the first sin ever committed against God. But in His love and grace, God knows you, comes to you, calls you out of hiding, and sets you free.

What are you still trying to hide? What in your life, if found out, would make you feel completely vulnerable and exposed—naked, like Adam and Eve in the garden?

It's just as pointless for you to think you can hide anything from God as it was for Adam and Eve to literally hide from Him behind a tree. How crazy is it to act as if the all-powerful Creator doesn't know where you are or what you're doing? God, the One who made you and knows everything about you, is inviting you out of the darkness and into the light.

No more hiding. No more blaming. No more faking that you don't need grace. God is calling you to a better life. Be free.

reflect

Pretending to have it all together and all figured out is exhausting. And it's a lie. No matter what picture-perfect images you project of your life, filtered and cropped to remove any imperfections, that's just not real life. What if you got honest about your need for grace? What freedom would exist if you didn't feel the pressure to prove yourself to God or others? Reflect on what you can do to start living in the freedom of Christ.

Take a few minutes to read Romans 8, an amazing chapter on your freedom as a child of God.

two
FAMILY IS MORE THAN JUST A NAME
read

The Bible is clear that by God's gracious love, you aren't just called a child of God. You *are* His child. He's your Father. This is more than just nice, religious language. This is fact. This is family:

> See what kind of love the Father has given to us, that
> we should be called children of God; and so we are.
> **1 JOHN 3:1**

This isn't religious effort or prideful posturing. This is a brand-new identity. You don't try to be part of a family. You just are. You did nothing to deserve it or earn it. There are only two ways a child can be part of a family: birth and adoption. The Bible includes both ideas when describing your relationship with the Heavenly Father.

Read 1 John 5:1.

What does this verse say about being born into God's family?

Read John 1:12-13.

What do these verses say about being born into God's family?

Read Ephesians 1:5.

What does this verse say about your adoption into God's family?

Read Romans 8:15.

What does this verse say about your adoption into God's family?

At the time these Scriptures were written, some people thought their relationship with God was completely tied to the family they were physically born into. Central to Jewish culture was the nation's identity as God's people. And God did have a special relationship with these people. He promised to make Abraham's family a great nation (see Genesis 12:1-3), and Abraham's grandson was named Israel. God kept this promise, which ultimately pointed to Jesus, God with us, born of a young Jewish girl who was engaged to a descendant of Israel's greatest king, David (see Matthew 1:1-16).

The idea of inheriting a relationship with God still exists today, though it becomes less popular as our culture identifies less and less with religion. You may have even said something like this before: "Sure, I'm a Christian. I went to church sometimes with my parents or my grandma. I'm not some other religion. So I'm a Christian, I guess."

But the Scriptures you read are clear that a personal relationship with God isn't determined by where you were born as the result of a physical act but by the deliberate act of your Heavenly Father's will for you to be born again spiritually. That's a point Jesus made in His conversation with Nicodemus, the religious leader born into the right Jewish family (see John 3:1-21). John 1:12-13 and 1 John 5:1 also make it clear that being born into God's family is completely tied to our belief in Jesus, the Son of God. This is a result of the Father's will, not our own. Nobody wills himself or herself to be born. Nobody chooses when or where he or she will be born.

Likewise, nobody chooses to be adopted. This is also an act of the Father's will. He chooses you. Don't miss that. There are no accidents in the family of God. Human parents may not plan on the birth of a child and may not know what to do, but your Heavenly Father has a plan for every person He created. He knew exactly who you would be, when and where and to whom you would be born, and how He would adopt you into His family.

In contrast to the idea that a relationship with God is tied to the family you are born into, some people think they could never have a relationship with God because of the situation they were born into. In New Testament times Gentiles were "the others." They were everybody else—non-Jewish people. The Jews were God's people. Everybody else wasn't. If you've ever felt you weren't entitled to a relationship with God or you're in His family by default, this idea probably resonates with you: "God would never love me. He wouldn't choose me. He wants other people. The people who do all those religious things. Since He knows what I've done, where I've been, and who I really am, then a relationship with Him is impossible. If He's real, He's not paying any attention to my life."

But God chose us in Christ. He has a purpose and a plan for each person. We weren't His people, but now we are (see 1 Peter 2:9-10). It's not about us—who we are or where we were born. It's about a loving Father who pursues us. Chooses us. Loves us. Unconditionally.

Children adopted into a family have every right possessed by the children born into the family. They enjoy every provision, protection, blessing, and inheritance of the Father. No matter who the child was before, now they bear the Father's name.

Which of these sentiments do you most relate to: feeling entitled to a relationship with God or feeling unworthy to be His child?

How do these biblical descriptions of being born again and adopted into God's family make you feel? How do they free you from your efforts and failures?

How does knowing that God chose you and has a plan give you hope for a future, regardless of your past or present?

It's a beautiful picture in Scripture: God extends His love and family to include whoever believes in Him. Your flesh and blood don't determine your eternal relationship with the Heavenly Father. Jesus gave His body and blood on the cross so that you could have a new life as part of God's family.

Paul wrote to the Gentile believers in Ephesus, who were likely former idol worshipers:

> Now in Christ Jesus you who once were far off have been brought near by the blood of Christ. For he himself is our peace, who has made us both one and has broken down in his flesh the dividing wall of hostility.
> **EPHESIANS 2:13-14**

We're not enemies with God; we're friends. We're not strangers; we're family.

Being a Christian is more than just a name. It's a new identity. It's a relationship. It's an eternal inheritance.

The blood Jesus shed is greater than the blood in your veins. You've been made part of His family. Forever.

reflect

Take time to be in awe of the truth that you're known and loved by God. Reflect on the fact that you're a child of God—by the grace of His will. Praise Him. Thank Him. Express your love for your Heavenly Father. Consider that living in relationship with a loving Heavenly Father and following His Son are different from just calling yourself a Christian. Let this truth change your life.

three
FAILURE DOESN'T EQUAL FIRING
read

Jesus told His followers they weren't His servants—they weren't employees doing an assigned task—but they were His friends (see John 15:15). He chose them so that they could experience the Father's love. Jesus brought a group of normal people the world would have never chosen, with all their failures and flaws, into an intimate relationship. He knew them, and they knew Him.

The same is true for you today. Jesus knows you. You can know Him. You have a personal relationship. You're not a servant blindly following instructions. You're part of something bigger and better than that. You can experience the life-changing love of the Father and share it with the world.

What feelings or attitudes result when you view your relationship with Jesus as similar to an employer and employee?

What do you currently view in your Christian life as a task, duty, or job assignment?

How does the idea of love and relationship change the perception of being an impersonal servant of God?

It's true that Jesus said our actions are an important part of our relationship with the Father. Scripture says obedience to the Father is an act of love and trust, revealing our identity as His children (see 1 John 5:3). But it isn't the begrudging duty of a reluctant employee. It's an act of faith in the One who proves Himself always faithful and infinitely greater than anything in this world. We believe our Father knows what's best for our lives, so we obey.

One of the most famous biblical stories about the unconditional love of a father for his child is found in the Gospel of Luke. Jesus told a parable illustrating just how great the bond of family is and how we all seem to misunderstand the nature of a relationship with our

Heavenly Father. In the story of the prodigal son, the father didn't owe either son anything. Both sons acted ungratefully toward the Father's love in different ways. But one son came to his senses.

Read Luke 15:11-32.

In what ways have you acted ungratefully toward God, your Heavenly Father?

Are you more like the wild, rebellious child or the proud, entitled child?

Why do you relate to that character in Jesus' story?

Both sons failed to appreciate their relationship with the father. But their failure didn't change the facts. The fact was that they were family. They were children of the father. They were in covenant—which is based on promise, not performance. Their behavior and attitude didn't change that.

The facts were greater than their feelings.

Their father was greater than their failure.

The covenant was greater than a contract.

The sons' failures didn't bring the relationship with their father to an end. The father disregarded the repentant son's request to be made a servant, so the boy wasn't demoted. He wasn't sent away. He wasn't fired, because he wasn't an employee. Neither can you be fired because of your failure, because you aren't an employee. You're a child of the Father, of the King. And His love for you is extravagant and unconditional. Nothing changes that. Not a bad day. Not a bad attitude.

You're accepted. Embraced. Your return is always celebrated.

Read Romans 8:35-39.

What in your life (past or present) seems unforgivable? What have you felt was separating you from the love of Jesus?

Romans 8 explains that as part of God's family, the Spirit of Jesus constantly works to bring us life, freedom, and forgiveness. No matter how it may seem—good or bad—God uses everything to grow us up as His children, making us more and more like Jesus. Even growing pains are still signs of growth. He promises to finish the good work He has begun in you (see Philippians 1:6). He's not done with you.

Your identity as a child of the Father doesn't change. The good news of the gospel doesn't change either. No matter what you do or how you feel, the gospel is still the gospel. And you don't stop needing the gospel just because you've put your faith in Jesus and been adopted by the Father. The gospel is more than good news that redeems you once. The gospel continues to be good news that restores you when you stumble each day:

> If we say we have no sin, we deceive ourselves, and the truth is not in us. If we confess our sins, he is faithful and just to forgive us our sins and to cleanse us from all unrighteousness.
> **1 JOHN 1:8-9**

What do you need to confess right now?

Know that confession brings freedom and restoration. The Father celebrates and blesses the child who turns from selfish attitudes to receive the joy of being in a right relationship with Him. You can't clean yourself up after wallowing with pigs. Only Jesus can make you clean. He promises to wash you clean from all stubborn sin. Pride is filthy. It only drives you away from the heart of your Father. But when you humble yourself, you realize He has open arms that are ready to embrace you.

You were lost, but now you're found. Repent, turn around, come to your senses, return to the Father, and enjoy celebrating life with Him.

The Father's faithfulness is greater than your failures.

reflect

Psalm 13:5-6 describes God's love as unfailing, faithful, or steadfast. As you read these verses, allow yourself to feel overwhelmed by the Father's love, grace, mercy, forgiveness, and joy for you as His child. Express your heart in confession, humility, and the security of your identity in Christ.

WORSHIP
>RITUALS

start

WELCOME EVERYONE AND START BY REVIEWING SESSION 4 BEFORE INTRODUCING SESSION 5.

Session 4 focused on freedom, family, and failure.

What was most helpful, encouraging, or challenging from your personal reading and reflection in session 4?

Today we'll look at the practice of worship.

What do you think of when you hear the word *worship?*

There are certain elements or rituals that may be included in worship, but worship is more than just doing something at a certain time or place. Keep the following question in mind as we watch the next video.

If Jesus > religion, what does it mean to worship Him?

watch

USE THESE STATEMENTS TO FOLLOW ALONG AS YOU WATCH "WORSHIP > RITUALS."

When you're invested in something and it gets damaged, you want to restore it—all of it.

The minute you start following Jesus, you go into ministry.

Ministry is taking your domain and engaging the world with that.

Every square inch of the earth is God's, and He wants us to take part with Him in restoring it.

Worship is an affection of your heart. Everyone worships.

Nothing is inherently evil, but are we going to align ourselves with the way God created things to work in their proper place? Are we going to worship Him or other things?

In Jesus, when you trust Him, you become the true temple.

Jesus said we should worship in spirit and truth, but we often have one without the other.

A lot of us think of God's will as a dot—one perfect plan for our life—and if we miss that dot, we're out of His will. But the Bible describes God as a loving Father, and Fathers set loving parameters for children—like a circle with room to grow and freedom to explore.

All of life is worship. What are you worshiping?

SCRIPTURES: 2 Corinthians 5:18-19; Genesis 1; 2:15; Exodus 20:3-5; John 4:20-24; 1 Corinthians 6:19; 10:31; 12:4; 2 Corinthians 6:16; 1 Timothy 4:4; Matthew 7:11; 28:19; Revelation 21:10

Video sessions available at
www.lifeway.com/JesusIsGreater

respond

USE THESE STATEMENTS AND QUESTIONS TO GUIDE A GROUP DISCUSSION.

What have you lived for in the past?

Where else do people seek meaning and purpose in life?

When have you wondered or even worried about God's will?

How has seeing God's will as a dot or a circle affected you and your view of God?

How do our previous discussions about freedom and God as a loving Father help you understand that His will is more like the boundaries of a circle than a precise point we have to get right?

We can overcomplicate God's will and what's right, holy, or considered ministry. God's will is specific about our general purpose but allows freedom in the practical, everyday details.

Read 2 Corinthians 5:18-19.

What do these verses identify as God's general will for our lives?

Read 1 Corinthians 6:19-20 and 2 Corinthians 6:16.

How does being the temple influence the way you see your life?

What does it mean not to be your own?

How does being the temple shape your understanding of worship?

Read 1 Corinthians 10:31.

What do you like to do?

How can you worship God in that pursuit? How can you share the gospel and advance the Kingdom with that activity?

WRAP UP WITH PRAYER. ENCOURAGE EVERYONE TO COMPLETE THE PERSONAL READING & REFLECTION ON THE FOLLOWING PAGES BEFORE YOUR NEXT GROUP SESSION.

PERSONAL READING & REFLECTION

WORSHIP > RITUALS

What is worship? What is good and holy? What should we do to honor God and please Him? How can we know His will? We overcomplicate the answers to these questions with formulas, checklists, or categories. But following Jesus isn't some kind of secret code to unlock by performing the right sequence of steps. You don't have to prove your devotion or earn bonus points from Him to reach the next level in life.

Scripture assures us that when we want God more than anything else, He will give us the desires of our hearts (see Psalm 37:4). If everything God created is good, then we don't need to segregate secular from sacred. To be a good Christian, you don't have to buy only Christian things, go to Christian schools, or get Christian jobs (all those things may be good for you but aren't required). You were created unique, in the image of God. So do whatever you do, wherever you are, for the glory of God. Everything can be an act of worship, not just certain activities during a scheduled time at a certain location. Worship is more than a religious service. Worship is the way you live. Live intentionally and creatively to honor Christ.

Three ideas can help us wrap our hearts and minds around the fact that all of life is worship:

1. **Your calling is more than a career.**
2. **God's will is more like a circle than a dot.**
3. **Whom we worship is greater than where we worship.**

For even more, read chapter 9 in the book *Jesus>Religion.*

one
CALLING IS MORE THAN A CAREER
read

Ever see or hear the word *vocation?*

That's a word we use today to describe a profession, right? We have vocational schools that focus on the development and mastery of technical skills and highly specialized knowledge related to a particular trade or career.

Engineers. Lawyers. Doctors. Mechanics. Plumbers. Ministers.

Vocation means *calling*. It even looks like the word *voice*. Before it grew to include any technical field, the roots of the word were in the Christian community. People felt a calling from God to devote their lives to full-time service of the church.

But even before that, *vocation* originally referred to God's calling people to salvation— bringing the dead to life. It was responding to God's invitation to join His family.

It was the voice of our Father calling His children into new life in relationship with Jesus.

Read 1 Peter 2:9-10.

Have you responded to God's initial calling out of darkness and into the light of His truth? If so, how did that change your life?

Do you feel a specific calling on your life? Are you drawn toward a specific career, cause, or area of interest?

How would you share that life-changing transformation with others in day-to-day life or through your specific interests?

A lot of people take the idea of being *holy,* which means *set apart for God,* and run to an extreme. They think being a good Christian means distancing themselves as far as possible from secular things and forming a weird little subculture—a Christian bubble.

Read John 17:15-21.

How is what Jesus prayed for His followers the opposite of a Christian-bubble mentality?

How can you be in the world but not of it—set apart for God's purposes but close to the people who need Jesus?

Often people think that to be a good Christian means you have to buy only Christian things, go to Christian schools, study Christian subjects, and even get Christian jobs. Maybe you've even wondered whether God was calling you into ministry. And yes, some people are definitely called into professional areas of service like preachers or missionaries (see Ephesians 4:11). But really, every Christian is in ministry. Our ministries just look different. Some are called to be Christian bakers, entrepreneurs, artists, educators, or stay-at-home parents. But no matter what specialty you're in, the work isn't exclusively Christian. The person doing it is a Christian.

Read 2 Corinthians 5:13-15.

If you've ever worried whether you'll look crazy doing what you love and really following Jesus 100 percent, be encouraged. Paul wrote that it's OK either to be misunderstood or to seem perfectly reasonable. Everybody isn't going to understand your decision to follow Jesus. But everyone should be able to see Jesus in you. Live your life for Him, no matter what you do or don't do.

Read 2 Corinthians 5:17-21.

How can you represent Jesus within your circle of influence?

Your calling is to know Jesus and to make Him known.

reflect

**What do you love? What are you good at? What interests you?
Express yourself in a way unique to how God has wired you.**

two
MORE LIKE A CIRCLE THAN A DOT
read

Do you have freedom to do what you want? Or does God have a plan for your life?

Yes.

God's will often feels like an elusive or confusing thing, and people generally fall toward one extreme end of the spectrum or the other in terms of how much they think about it. We may not think about God's will at all because we don't believe in God, don't believe He has a plan for our lives, or don't believe we could figure it out. He's too busy being the Supreme Being of the universe, doing God things, to worry about our mundane lives.

Or on the opposite end of the spectrum, we obsess over God's will, even to the point of being paralyzed with fear—scared to step out of bounds. We fear that if we make the wrong choice, God will punish us for being out of His will. Every detail becomes a matter of right and wrong: God's perfect will or utter sin. Life then becomes like walking through a field of land mines, each step an act of faith that you desperately hope doesn't blow up in your face. One wrong decision could have brutal consequences.

On a scale of 0 to 10, how often do you think about God's will for your life?

0	1	2	3	4	5	6	7	8	9	10
Never										Obsessively

Read Romans 12:2.

What does this verse say about knowing God's will?

Read Romans 8:26-29.

What do these verses add to your understanding of your ability to know God's will?

Paul wrote to the Christians in Rome some beautiful, rich descriptions of our relationship with God and His will for us in Jesus.

Not only is it possible to know God's will, but God also wants us to know His will. In fact, He helps us know His will through the work of the Holy Spirit. Paul wrote that sometimes we don't even know what to pray for, but the Spirit of God, who knows our hearts and God's heart, serves as the perfect intercessor between us (see Romans 8:26-27).

God isn't a distant or cruel deity playing hide-and-seek or guessing games.

Paul clarified the heart of God's good, pleasing, and perfect will for your life: for you to be conformed to the image of His Son, Jesus (see verse 29). God's will is for you to become a part of His family and grow to be more and more like Jesus.

What else does Scripture reveal about the will of God? We're going to look at a lot of Scriptures today because they're all too good to miss. Besides salvation, experiencing God's will is possibly the most freeing and joy-giving truth in life. It's a game changer.

Read John 6:29.

What does this verse say is God's will for you?

Read 1 Thessalonians 4:3.

What does this verse say is God's will for you?

Read 1 Thessalonians 5:18.

What does this verse say is God's will for you?

Read 1 Peter 2:15.

What does this verse say is God's will for you?

Too often we overcomplicate God's will for our lives. We think of God's will as a dot requiring pinpoint accuracy. But thinking of His will more like a circle fits the descriptions of God's will mentioned in Scripture. God isn't a tyrant. He's a loving Father. And when we keep that in mind, His will isn't something to be scared of but trusted. Seeking God's will doesn't oppress and restrict but gives freedom and joy. Religion makes life impossibly difficult because no one can live up to an acceptable standard (see Matthew 23:3-4). But Jesus comes alongside you and offers a better life (see Matthew 11:28-30).

You don't search for God's will in your own strength. Jesus is walking with you, doing the heavy lifting, so that you can experience the abundant life your Father desires for you.

Read Psalm 37:3-4.

If God's will is a circle, how would you explain the Lord's promise to give you the desires of your heart?

You're a unique child of God. Fathers have great joy in seeing their children filled with joy and fully alive. As the perfect Father, God wants you to grow and express yourself within the healthy boundaries He has provided in love and wisdom. Doing God's will is a natural part of being in God's family (see Mark 3:35). When your desires become the same as God's desires, He gladly gives you what you want and need—more of Him. He's what is best. He's most satisfying. When you want Him more than anything else, everything you do within the circle God has drawn becomes an act of worship. Everything in the circle is Christian and holy. There's no more anxiety about the fine line between secular and sacred.

Paul put it this way:

> I appeal to you therefore, brothers, by the mercies of God, to present your bodies as a living sacrifice, holy and acceptable to God, which is your spiritual worship.
> **ROMANS 12:1**

> Whatever you do, in word or deed, do everything in the name of the Lord Jesus, giving thanks to God the Father through him.
> **COLOSSIANS 3:17**

God wants more for you. More joy. More freedom. More life. He wants to make you more like Jesus.

reflect

Draw a circle that fills this page. Around the circle write the phrases you identified from Scriptures that describe God's will (page 85). Inside the circle write all the things you're trying to choose among. If they encourage you to grow in all the ways written around the circle, keep them. If they don't, cross them out. Find joy and confidence in the freedom that lies within God's will for you.

three

WHOM WE WORSHIP IS GREATER THAN WHERE WE WORSHIP

read

Worship is more than gathering at a designated time and place and using a certain style of music. I really don't think Jesus has a preference about an organ and stained glass or a band and lights. It's not about when, where, or how we worship; it's about whom we worship. It's about the posture of our hearts. It's about lifting up the name of Jesus as our ultimate desire.

You may have a worship style that's most natural for expressing yourself. That's cool. It's a good thing to be fully engaged in worship and surrounded by a community of brothers and sisters in Christ. Just remember that it's not a show. It's not about impressing you or other people; it's about glorifying Him.

What helps you focus your heart and mind on Jesus in worship?

It's easy to forget that worship is all about Jesus. Worship isn't about our preferences or convenience. It's not about being better than another group of people who do things differently or meet somewhere else. To discover what kind of worship really honors Jesus, let's revisit His encounter with the woman at the well.

Read John 4:19-26.

Jesus was saying that with His life, death, and resurrection as the promised Messiah—the Savior of God's people—everything we thought we knew about worship changed. Worship isn't about holy spots but holy lives.

What debates or preferences distract you from worshiping in spirit and truth?

If this idea of worship is hard to distinguish from just singing, praying, or other rituals in a religious service or ceremony, think of it this way. Worship is defined by glory and thanksgiving. We're worshiping when we give glory to something, when we give ultimate value to something. This can be a job, a relationship, pleasure, anything. And whatever we give glory to, we're willing to sacrifice for. Remember that Paul said we become living sacrifices; our lives become acts of worship (see Romans 12:1). Every breath is a song.

As true worshipers, worshiping in spirit and in truth, we become the temple. We're the place of worship. We're where God can be experienced. Paul made this clear in his letter to the Christians in Corinth:

> Do you not know that you are God's temple
> and that God's Spirit dwells in you?
> **1 CORINTHIANS 3:16**

Read 1 Corinthians 6:19-20.

In your own words, how would you explain the idea of a temple in general and what it means to be God's temple?

How does viewing yourself as God's temple shape your understanding of worship?

What decisions, habits, or lifestyles would you change in light of the fact that your body is God's temple?

The presence of your holy Creator and Savior is with you right now. In this very moment. Let that sink in. Jesus, Immanuel, God with us—this is more than just a name. He's with you. Literally. Powerfully. And He alone is worthy of all praise, honor, and glory.

In the account of creation, Adam and Eve were in the garden, where God walked among them. He called them out of hiding, provided for them after their sin, and began the long process of restoration. From Genesis to Revelation is the sweeping narrative of redemption in which everything is being set free from the slavery and death of sin through the love and grace of God through Jesus Christ. The Book of Revelation provides a sneak peak at the other end of the story. In the end Christ will restore everything, set it right again, remake heaven and earth, and again dwell among His people.

Read Revelation 21:1-7.

According to these verses, why is Jesus worthy of your worship?

Jesus is the Alpha and Omega. That's the Greek alphabet's equivalent of saying He's the A through Z. He's the first, last, and everything in between. He's what life is all about. For Jesus to say He's the Alpha and Omega isn't proud boasting; it's simple fact. It's like putting your name, height, and eye color on a driver's license. Alpha and Omega are descriptions of who He really is. Jesus existed before He created everything, and He will live eternally after the world as we know it is gone.

For Jesus to desire your worship, devotion, and affection isn't egotistical or vain. It's actually an act of love. He desires what's best for you. He came to give you abundant and eternal life. To give our ultimate devotion and affection to anything other than Jesus always steals, kills, and destroys the abundance found only in a relationship with Him (see John 10:10). It's in your best interest to worship Him. He knows better than you do. He can provide better than you can. He can completely satisfy you in ways nothing in this world can. He gives joy and peace as nothing else can.

In the end, when everything is made new and we live forever in perfect peace, there will be no more temple. Everything will be consumed by the presence of God, and all glory will belong to Him. When reality is in perfect rhythm, glory won't be given to anything other than Him:

> I saw no temple in the city, for its temple
> is the Lord God the Almighty and the Lamb.
> **REVELATION 21:22**

But until that time, you're the temple. Everything you do is an act of worship, giving glory to Jesus or to something infinitely less worthy—which is idolatry and sin. Your body is the holy place where the presence and power of a holy God dwell on earth.

In the words of Paul:

> From him and through him and to him are
> all things. To him be glory forever. Amen.
> **ROMANS 11:36**

Jesus is worthy of more than just songs, buildings, and events. Your life is your worship of Him. Be holy because He is holy.

reflect

Spend a few minutes (or more) filling your heart and mind with the greatness of God and the amazing reality that His Spirit lives in you. You may want to use a concordance to find attributes of God, Jesus, and the Holy Spirit. You may simply want to fill this page with praise. You may want to go somewhere and praise Him while surrounded by the beauty of His creation. Worship Him, remembering that He's with you every moment.

COMMUNITY
>CONFORMITY

start

WELCOME EVERYONE TO YOUR FINAL SESSION. START BY REVIEWING SESSION 5 BEFORE INTRODUCING SESSION 6.

Session 5 focused on your calling, God's will, and worship.

What was most helpful, encouraging, or challenging from your personal reading and reflection in session 5?

Today we'll look at life in community, a word that comes from the word *common*.

What do you share in common with people in this group?

What differences do you have from people in this group?

In Jesus what we have in common is greater than our differences. That idea is at the heart of community. The unity and diversity of the church should be a beautiful reality. Unfortunately, church is one of the most misunderstood aspects of a relationship with Jesus today.

Each session of this Bible study was intended to help us set aside preconceived ideas and experiences with religion so that we could gain a clearer picture of Jesus, the Bible, worship, holiness, and our purpose in life. Keep the following question in mind as we watch the final video.

If Jesus > religion, why is the church so important?

watch

USE THESE STATEMENTS TO FOLLOW ALONG AS YOU WATCH "COMMUNITY > CONFORMITY."

You were created for community. You were created to be in the family of God.

The church is a vehicle—God's agent—to reconcile the world to Himself.

The diversity of the early church was as scandalous community like the world had never seen.

The mission we've been given is to make disciples, engage the world, and worship God.

How is Jesus going to show Himself in the world? Through His body—which is us.

Jesus makes us family, even when everything else about us is very different.

Community is not country-club, cookie-cutter conformity. It's being unified in diversity.

You are valuable; the church body needs you.

The church isn't optional. You can't have Jesus without the church. It's the bride and body of Jesus.

The church doesn't exist for itself.

SCRIPTURES: Genesis 1:26; 2 Corinthians 5:19-20; Matthew 16:18; Acts 2:37-47; Galatians 3:28; 6:2; 1 Corinthians 12:4-6,12-20,25-26; Ephesians 2:13; 4:15; 5:25-27; Romans 12:10; Hebrews 10:24-25; Revelation 19:7

Video sessions available at
www.lifeway.com/JesusIsGreater

respond

USE THESE STATEMENTS AND QUESTIONS TO GUIDE A GROUP DISCUSSION.

Jefferson opened by saying that by God's design we're created for community.

To which illustration do you best relate and why?
□ Life without community is like life without oxygen.
□ Life without community is like sitting on a one-legged stool.
□ Life in community is like a family.
□ Life in community is like a forest.

Read 1 Corinthians 12:4-6,12-20,25-26 and Galatians 3:28.

What encouragement does Paul's description of diversity and unity give you as part of Jesus' body—His church?

As a valuable part of the body, how have you experienced growth through the church? Or if not involved, where could you plug in?

Read Romans 12:10; Galatians 6:2; and Hebrews 10:24-25.

What actions are explicitly taught in each of these verses as characteristic of true Christian community?

When and how have you experienced any of these actions?

How can this group help you or others in any of these areas?

Read Matthew 16:13-18.

Various opinions have always existed about Jesus' identity. Confessing the truth of Jesus as the Christ, the Son of God, is the common ground on which the church is built.

How would you explain to someone who Jesus is?

How has this study helped you know and love Jesus more?

WRAP UP WITH PRAYER. ENCOURAGE EVERYONE TO COMPLETE THE PERSONAL READING & REFLECTION TO CONCLUDE THIS STUDY. DECIDE AS A GROUP WHAT YOU WILL STUDY NEXT AND WHOM YOU WILL INVITE TO JOIN YOU.

PERSONAL READING & REFLECTION

COMMUNITY > CONFORMITY

Life shouldn't be lived alone. It's better together. And while we've seen that religious activities in and of themselves have no value, when Christ is the focus of our lives and the desire of our hearts, believers will be drawn together as a community to celebrate Him and to experience more of Him. Those activities aren't done to earn points with God but to express our thankfulness, joy, and love for Jesus, who unites us. If the church is the body and bride of Christ, then we can't love the Head without the body. A healthy church isn't a club for clones, forcing conformity. It's a vibrant and diverse community brought together by Jesus. And having Jesus in common is greater than any differences that exist among us. Individual members of the body are encouraged to love the community of Christ, joining other followers of Jesus so that the many parts can work together to grow to maturity and provide shelter for those who are hurting and in need.

Jesus' plan to share His love with the world is the church. The church isn't an institutional subculture that withdraws from the world but a light that engages the culture, offering the love and joy of Christ.

1. **Life is better together.**
2. **The body is more than any one part.**
3. **The light of Jesus is greater than darkness.**

For even more, read chapter 10 in the book *Jesus>Religion.*

one
LIFE IS BETTER TOGETHER
read

The narrative of Scripture begins with a beautiful rhythm in creation. God, the holy Trinity—Father, Son, and Holy Spirit—made everything from nothing. Light. Good. Sky and sea. Good. Land and everything that grows on it. Good. Orderly solar system. Good. Creatures swimming in the water and flying in the air. Good. Creatures living on dry land. Good.

Everything was good. The Hebrew language has a word for the peace and balance that characterized God's original creation: *shalom.* Harmony. Rhythm. Order. Everything was created in its place by design and with purpose.

Seven times God pronounced His creation "good," with the last description being "very good" (see Genesis 1:4,10,12,18,21,25,31). This "very good" came after the following:

> God said, "Let us make man in our image, after our likeness. And let them have dominion over the fish of the sea and over the birds of the heavens and over the livestock and over all the earth and over every creeping thing that creeps on the earth."
> So God created man in his own image,
> in the image of God he created him;
> male and female he created them.
> **GENESIS 1:26-27**

Look at those verses again. Circle every plural pronoun.

Why is it significant that God and people are relational beings?

The first time anything in Scripture is described as not good, even before sin entered the world, was when Adam was alone in the work God had given him. He needed community:

> The LORD God said, "It is not good that the man should be alone; I will make him a helper fit for him."
> **GENESIS 2:18**

God had just entrusted Adam with good work to do in His creation and had warned him about sin and death (see Genesis 2:15-17). Man and woman were designed as perfect counterparts, created in the glorious image of God and complementing each other in their work together. They enjoyed life together naked and unashamed, one flesh, and they had nothing to hide.

But the honeymoon was over in the next chapter. Together Adam and Eve gave in to temptation, desiring to choose right and wrong for themselves instead of trusting God. As a result, they went into hiding. They felt shame. Relationships were broken. Work became hard. Life became hard (see Genesis 3). But God called them out of hiding. And check this out. The original Greek word for *church* in the New Testament—*ekklesia*—literally means *people called out*.

The church is a community of people called out of sin and shame; called out of death and darkness; and given new life by the Father, Son, and Holy Spirit. The good order of creation is being restored in the community of those called out by God. Together we can resist sin and do the work of God as His image bearers in the world.

Life without community is like trying to sit on a stool with only one leg. It's exhausting and misses the point of the design. You were made for relationships with God and His people.

Jesus didn't leave us as orphans without a home and without hope (see John 14:1-18). We've been made part of His family. Our hope is in the gospel—the good news of Jesus. That's what we share as the common bond of Christian community. We aren't left to figure out good and evil, right and wrong, life and death on our own.

Read Hebrews 10:23-25.

What benefits of and instructions for community are described in these verses?

Read Romans 12:9-21.

What benefits of and instructions for community are described in these verses?

Why settle for anything less than life together in community?

reflect

What can you do to build community and show appreciation for the people in your life? Get creative. Go out of your way to build community, to invest in meaningful friendships, and to get involved in your local church.

two
THE BODY IS MORE THAN ONE PART
read

Remember the hand from *The Addams Family?* They called the hand Thing. Thing was a crazy, spiderlike character that ran around the house like a pet—just a hand. And then there was Cousin Itt, who looked like a walking haystack—just hair. All hair.

Almost two thousand years before the special effects and costume design of *The Addams Family,* the apostle Paul used equally ridiculous images in a few of his letters that are now in your Bible. The picture is both humorous and beautiful, convicting yet encouraging.

Read 1 Corinthians 12:12-20.

In your own words, what did Paul write in verses 12-13 about being a Christian?

What comes to mind when you think of a Christian?

What comes to mind when you think of a church member?

Are your two previous answers the same? Why or why not?

What encouragement does this image of the body parts give you, especially if you've ever felt you didn't fit in the church?

When we think of church, we often think of a building when we should think of a body. Our culture sees it as an organization, but the Bible says it's an organism. Religion turns it into a club when it's really about Christ. The church isn't about conformity but community.

Read 1 Corinthians 12:21-27.

Sometimes it's easy to think that we have to be exactly like everyone else. Or that good Christians are the ones preaching, singing, playing in the band, or leading Bible studies. We can slip back into the cycle of comparison and frustration, feeling we're not good enough or don't have the right personality and gifts.

Or on the other end of the spectrum, we can become proud and conceited, thinking since other people aren't exactly like us, they're not really Christians—or at least not very good ones. But Paul is clear that both views are not only unnatural but also absurd.

Not only do you fit in the church, but the church also needs you. Whatever part you are, the body works together and needs every member to be fully alive, healthy, and functional.

Read Romans 12:3-5.

> **Which extreme do you lean toward—feeling that you don't fit and aren't important to the church or feeling that others aren't good enough because your gifts are more important?**

> **How does Paul's teaching give you a healthy perspective on yourself and on others in the church?**

No matter who you are, what you've done, what you've suffered, or when you started following Jesus, you're valued. You're loved. You're unique. You're part of His body. You're fearfully and wonderfully made for a reason. God has a plan and a purpose for you. If this is something you wrestle with and struggle to believe, read Psalm 139:13-16 now.

Paul reminded the church in Ephesus that what they had in common was faith in Jesus (see Ephesians 3:6). They were united by the power of the gospel. This kind of unity was scandalous and revolutionary in the first century, and it still is today. At the time of Jesus and Paul, Jews and Gentiles, rich and poor, men and women, slave and free didn't come together as equals. Cultures throughout world history were littered with segregation, racism, and human efforts to distinguish themselves. Look around at your own school, workplace, community, and even church and ask how much has really changed. But the early church, the body of Christ, united all these seemingly unrelated and incompatible parts of society into one community. Jesus' blood gives life to every part of His body. The diversity of Christ's church is beautiful. It's a glorious preview of our eternal home in heaven (see Revelation 5:9-10).

What could you do to encourage more diversity in your church?

Read Ephesians 4:11-16.

What are the importance and purpose of diversity?

How have others helped you grow up spiritually?

Paul wrote that Jesus gave different people different gifts and abilities, different functions as parts of the body for the sake of everybody's benefit. You aren't gifted because you're Jesus' favorite, more special than everyone else. You're blessed to be a blessing. You're gifted to share your time, talent, abilities, and resources with others. The goal is a healthy, mature, growing body. Not only does the church need you, but you also need the church. It's a mutually beneficial relationship. So we have to learn to love one another:

> Put on then, as God's chosen ones, holy and beloved, compassionate hearts, kindness, humility, meekness, and patience, bearing with one another and, if one has a complaint against another, forgiving each other; as the Lord has forgiven you, so you also must forgive. And above all these put on love, which binds everything together in perfect harmony. And let the peace of Christ rule in your hearts, to which indeed you were called in one body. And be thankful. Let the word of Christ dwell in you richly, teaching and admonishing one another in all wisdom, singing psalms and hymns and spiritual songs, with thankfulness in your hearts to God.
> **COLOSSIANS 3:12-16**

In the previous verses circle every word that describes the attitudes and actions that should characterize the body of Christ.

You're part of something bigger than yourself. You matter.

reflect

Regardless of popular opinion and misunderstanding about what's meant by the phrase "Jesus is greater than religion," you can't be a Christian and hate the church or say you don't need it. You're part of the body. So it should be natural to take care of it and make sure it's healthy (see Ephesians 5:29-30). Reflect on what it means to be a part of the body of Jesus in this world.

three
LIGHT IS GREATER THAN DARKNESS
read

> The light shines in the darkness, and the darkness has not overcome it. The true light, which gives light to everyone, was coming into the world. He was in the world, and the world was made through him, yet the world did not know him. He came to his own, and his own people did not receive him. But to all who did receive him, who believed in his name, he gave the right to become children of God, who were born, not of blood nor of the will of the flesh nor of the will of man, but of God. And the Word became flesh and dwelt among us, and we have seen his glory, glory as of the only Son from the Father, full of grace and truth.
> **JOHN 1:5,9-14**

This is the gospel.

Jesus isn't just a good man, religious teacher, social activist, moral role model, or historical figure. He's the Son of the Father. He's God. He's the Creator of everything—including you. He has always existed. But He humbled Himself to become part of His own creation. He became a man. Fully human. Fully God. Light. Truth. Grace. In the flesh.

What darkness do you see in the world?

What hope and confidence do you find in knowing that darkness hasn't and can't overcome the light of Jesus?

No matter how bad things may get or how bad they feel, the darkness won't prevail. We know even in history's darkest hour, when Jesus was rejected and murdered by the very people He came to save, the darkness didn't win. Jesus let Himself be nailed to a cross. He hung and died. He was wrapped in grave clothes and laid in a tomb sealed by a gigantic stone. His dead body was guarded by Roman soldiers. But three days later on Sunday morning, Jesus was alive. Resurrected. Glorious. The light pierced the darkness.

Think about it from a purely literal and scientific perspective. Darkness doesn't dim light. Light affects darkness. Chases it away. Darkness is simply an absence of light. It's technically impossible for darkness to overcome light. Darkness can't do anything to light except exist where there's no light.

If there are sketchy, shadowy places and dark closets in your life, let the Light in. Let Jesus transform every part of your life. You already know there's no real hiding from the Creator.

Light always wins. The darkness is losing.

Read John 8:12.

What promise does Jesus make to His followers?

Jesus said He's the Light and you're the light:

> As long as I am in the world, I am the light of the world.
> **JOHN 9:5**

> You are the light of the world.
> **MATTHEW 5:14**

How can both of these verses be true?

Read Matthew 5:14-16.

There's no hiding the reality of Jesus inside you. A city on a hill can't be hidden when its light is shining in the night sky. Even a tiny spark lights up darkness. The deeper the darkness, the more noticeable the light, and the bigger difference even a small light makes.

Christianity isn't as individualistic as some people want you to believe. Yes, your faith is personal; it has to be. It's a personal relationship with Jesus. But it isn't private. Jesus is the Light of the world. There's no hiding that and keeping it to yourself once His Spirit empowers you to light up the darkness.

How have you hidden the light of Jesus, keeping it private?

If Jesus really is all the things we've seen over the past six weeks, then you have to make a decision. Regardless of what anyone else believes, you have to decide what you believe about Jesus. This is the same thing He challenged His own disciples to do.

Read Matthew 16:13-18.

In your own words, who do you say Jesus is? What would you tell people about the person of Jesus?

Jesus is building His church on this confession of faith, by the grace of the Father. He promises that the gates of hell won't prevail against the church (see verse 18). Death and hell are as dark as it gets. And Jesus promises that the darkness won't overcome you as His follower. In fact, like darkness, gates don't actually do anything. Gates are defensive. They're meant to stop intruders.

Jesus expects and empowers you, as the light of the world, to storm the gates of hell, rescuing those hopelessly lost and trapped in sin who don't know the truth of the gospel.

You have a mission. You're God's plan A. There's no plan B.

You don't go to church. You _are_ the church. You're the light of the world. And the darkness is losing.

reflect

Whom do you know who needs Jesus? What will you do to shine the light of truth in the darkness? Reflect on the great hope that's in you and identify the people around you who need it too.

BONUS

If you didn't watch "The Story Behind the Video" when you read the introduction (or if you did but could use a refresher), watch it now at *www.lifeway.com/JesusIsGreater* or on the DVD in *Jesus > Religion DVD Bible Study Kit.*

In the video Jefferson explains how this Bible study you've just completed began with a poem he wrote for an open-mic night in his senior year of college, "Why I Hate Religion but Love Jesus," which subsequently went crazy viral. He had been hosting a small Bible study on campus but wanted to reach out to the people around him on their turf. In the video he encourages you to simply be faithful with the abilities, opportunities, and relationships God has given you and leave the rest up to Him.

ON THE PREVIOUS PAGES YOU'VE ALREADY IDENTIFIED PEOPLE IN YOUR LIFE AND THINGS YOU LOVE TO DO. NOW USE THESE FINAL PAGES TO CONSIDER WAYS YOU CAN SHARE JESUS IN YOUR SPHERE OF INFLUENCE AND DAILY ROUTINE.

Where do you go on a regular basis? Record your usual schedule.

What does being faithful look like in your sphere of influence?

Prayerfully brainstorm ways you can naturally, creatively, and intentionally share the incomparable joy and life-changing hope of Jesus in the everyday rhythm of your life.